DISOBEDIENCE

DISOBEDIENCE

writing from a bad time and place

BRITTNY BARONA

DISOBEDIENCE
WRITING FROM A BAD TIME AND PLACE

iUniverse books may be ordered through booksellers or by contacting:

iUniverse
1663 Liberty Drive
Bloomington, IN 47403
www.iuniverse.com
844-349-9409

ISBN: 978-1-6632-2043-1 (sc)
ISBN: 978-1-6632-2044-8 (e)

Print information available on the last page.

iUniverse rev. date: 04/20/2021

to those, like me, who live out of spite

CHAPTER 1

memories of the past

* * *

we were told to walk

on the

moon

I asked to stay on

earth

from solid ground

I could keep everyone

safe.

my classmates:

astronauts

I, keeping them safe

from home.

on a playground

haven't felt a burn

like that in quite a

while

a fossil of memories past

underneath the blazing sun

don't forget to hydrate

where's your dad?

he lost the keys and yelled

at you.

can't have fun in the

day at the park.

❋ ❋ ❋

People keep trying to mess with me.

Seeing things others don't see.

It almost makes me cry,

How they wish for me to die.

Don't tell me it'll pass.

I'm not a stupid ass.

It has always happened.

I feel mishapened.

Don't say to be cool,

I'm not a fool.

Don't tell me to stay,

For I'm running away.

(6th period Language Arts)

✾ ✾ ✾

I wish you could understand
Maybe hold my hand.
And save me when I fall.
It would help us all.

I want you to get over her.
It was you whom she lured
Into her steel trap.
You put up with all that crap.

I just want to see you happy,
make sure you are never snappy.
sorry for making you feel bad.
Forevermore, it'll be me sad.

(4:25pm at home after school)

＊　＊　＊

Your rejection

Made me feel I will never be perfection.

Your hurtful word

Lets compliments be unheard

My stupidity

makes me want to leave this city

And never return.

That lesson I have learned.

I know I have low self-esteem.

Yet this irony interacts with this theme.

Maybe I just want to die.

You'll never have to see me cry.

(after walking home from middle school)

＊ ＊ ＊

I really don't understand you

I'm not sure what you're saying is true.

As long as you're willing,

let it be the truth you're telling.

I'm very confused,

by what you're saying; it's been used.

I'll know if you say a lie,

for they'll cover you up to the sky.

I need to figure this out.

But I am full of doubt.

Your help is really needed.

I'll know if I'm misleaded.

(people keep saying I'm weird)

* * *

Why are you in this mess?

Weren't you told to remain less?

Your lesson is unlearned,

You're soon to be burned.

I've told you enough already

to stay still and steady.

And you had to be a fool,

to break up every rule.

And if that isn't enough,

You continue to act tough!

Please take good care,

for I will not be there.

(we haven't learned to be careful)

They all can just go to hell,

See me here, I am well.

They all can suck my dick,

Go ahead, call me spic.

I want to be left along

Hope my face is never shown

I just want to go away

I have absolutely nothing to say

Say what you want, I don't care

I'll just pull out all your hair.

Say what you need to say

I'll be better than you one day.

(8th period Social Studies)

he wasn't even to the top of the

    fence before he collapsed

his body crumbling with the help

    of gravity and the drugs in his system

the circle we made around him splatters

    of red, we made sure to keep our

    shoes clean

his eyes met mine. soulless

    i felt

        fear

            after that I can't

              remember

              a thing

✳ ✳ ✳

Did you see my fury right before it faded?

Did you feel the hidden hatred in my words?

Didn't you see my fingers curled into fist,

Nails slowly sharpen, cuts upon my wrists?

Didn't you say that I'd never make it?

Your negative views are obviously ignored.

Didn't you notice my feelings weren't legit?

And that you always had me bored.

I HATE THIS! I hate all of it!

Why can't you see that I am angry!

I hate this! Why can't you see?

You're killing me slowly!

Why don't you understand.

✻ ✻ ✻

You ask me to turn in my work
You tell me to put my phone away
You say, "any questions" but don't
care for what we have to say

When I stand up I'm disrupting your class
but you pick up your phone and blab away
when I don't understand something,
you'll call me out, that's really not okay

But now that I have your attention
I believe your mind won't think to stray
And maybe you will hear me out
and hear the stuff I can't say.

I wanted you to ask me Why I didn't do

the work you assigned instead instead of the typical

sigh. I wanted you to ask why the bags under my eyes got bigger and darker.

I wanted you to ask me how many hours

I slept last night and how many I

worked. I wanted you to ask me why the

gas dial has been on empty for the past

three months on the only way I get to

school.

As I look out from the doorway of the shelter I have made

I grin as I notice the game that nature has played

Mother Nature, a mom, has learned to tease

And fools us into doing things we wouldn't have pleased to do

Like stay indoors all day while the animals nap

When we'd rather be outside making a treasure map

Oh mother, my mother why do you make it rain

It seems as though the flowers have it all to gain

And I am left, shivering in a cave along

As I see the birds and they way they had flown

Okay, fine, you made the ground soft to sit on

The grass reminds me of an out-of-control lawn

But I'm begging of boredom, please stop the rain!

Before I count all of the raindrops and go insance!

You know what, fine, I'll run and get sick

By falling on wet grass, all wet and slick

Maybe then you'll send to bring out the sun

And then you'll notice I'm not the only one

Who wants to run outside, when it's warm!

And not in the cold we feel now.

How does the dagger feel now

when you're on the receiving end?

If this is what you call betrayal,

this is what I call revenge.

＊　＊　＊

cheek still burning

she felt the smoothness

of the pearls

clutched in her hand.

looks like she really did have money!

a few crushed beneath her heel.

i'm broken

don't try putting me

back together. you'll

just cut yourself on

the broken pieces of my heart.

＊　＊　＊

It'll take all the pain away

At least for a little while

Let me be for just a day

For once in my life let me smile

I promise I'll just take one

I'm not ready for the whole bottle

What I'm experiencing isn't fun

Turn on the bike, full throttle

Let's hope I don't crash

Will death be quick or slow?

All my life I learned to lash

Out and make a show

The knife is getting closer

How many cuts can you see?

Call my mom, and for me, tell her

That from my burden she is free

And now under the waves I go

Do you see the light?

No, air, even more so

I'm giving in, no fight...

✽ ✽ ✽

I don't want to think

I don't want to try

Let me waste away in fear

I don't want to care

I just need to cry

Just let me drown in my tears

How long has it been already

really only 2 days and you

still haven't have you

Or are your eyes still glazed

Well then let me tell you, what has

been going on. Better let me

show you all the scars I've got

Don't speak nor say a word

I swear I didn't feel pain

What you still assured?

Well, I don't care, I have nothing to gain

You now look at me, with some

kind of fear. You grab my hand and

whisper, lets get out of here. But

my smile so morbid makes you let

me go, You back away so slowly. wait.

You'll miss the show

do you remember when you used to

be mean to me? do you remember

how low my self esteem was growing up?

do you remember me crying at night

because you used to compare me

to my friends, telling me they

were better? I wrote down their

names and each slash on my arm

belongs to them, reminding me that

I'll never be good enough.

❋ ❋ ❋

I've called out

for help

I've held on to

life with clenched

fists, struggling

to survive

I reach out to

you when

I'm feeling bad

But why don't you

check on me

yourself?

* * *

ten minutes after

I dropped you off

at your job I

almost flipped the car

your words made my eyes

blind to the road, my

screams echoing back to me,

when I wiped my eyes and

turned the wheel, I almost

died.

I wish I had crashed.

Maybe you would finally be

nice to me.

※ ※ ※

blue

red

white

      flashes of light

gunshot

firecracker

hit on the head

      I don't like the 4th of July

I'd rather be

dead

asleep

in bed with headphones on.

✳ ✳ ✳

SHOES!

you made my phone ring

so much that day

and it was only because

you NEEDED to buy me

SHOES!

can't you just call me

to say you love me?

I don't want you to

waste your money on

something like

SHOES!

✳ ✳ ✳

If a body is just a reflection of the soul

I wonder what mine would look like

Would it be strong and sure or

small and weak like I am.

On the outside I act mature, I act as if

Nothing bothers me because If I pretend

it doesn't hurt maybe it won't. Just a skin

hides my thoughts of bitterness that plagues

my dreams, turning them into nightmares.

Those nightmares haunt my waking hour and

I feel as though I can't be anything. The

hopes that lived as long as I have seemed to

abandon me, leaving me way behind as I

struggle to keep up, shouting at them to wait.

I'm being held back by my insecurities, my family,

my past, my doubts. Hope isn't waiting for me.

They've left to look for someone with less

bitterness in their heart. Leaving me behind.

* * *

who are you

    when did you change

    why have you allowed your bitterness to

POISON

    the ones who need you most

when you look in a mirror, do you hate what

    you see?

        is that why you take it all out on

ME?

you swear and curse, "I don't need you at all"

    am I only of value to you when

        I'm quiet

        obedient

        hurt?

your one duty is to protect the very

    beings you brought into

    this world

why am I doing your job for you.

a well behaved child is a

baby ignored. a

spank with too much force,

the invasion of privacy,

isolated and alone,

demanded to be the best,

punished for it all, a

trauma ridden teen, a

semi-functioning adult.

obedient. observant.

    don't open your

mouth. it becomes a

bigger

    target.

* * *

why don't I know all of

my own history?

some memories faded,

others altered by future

thoughts

I need to know the truth

so that I may be able

to live.

✿ ✿ ✿

we were told to build castles of sand

you were given a shovel I was

lead by hand to the

sea

"try to build it as best as you can"

what am I supposed to do but

drown I have to try to get out

of this water

"no, build your castle where you are"

they guard the shore, no way to

get in, I see you working hard

please help me

CHAPTER 2

eight years gone

✳ ✳ ✳

I haven't written in a long time

My feelings have been purged

No bad feelings we don't want to

die

The way my art is now to

what it was before, why

didn't anyone check on me, I was more than willing to

die

had it not been for you, my

steady foundation keeping me in check

keeping me accountable, making sure the nails didn't pierce enough for me to

die

You aren't around anymore

I've learned to hate you and everyday

I miss you, I wish you fought for us the way you fought for me to stay

alive.

* * *

he was never a good

friend to you but

you kept him around

because you grew up together

you realized way too

late that his only

intention was to

fuck you over.

why didn't you listen to

me

* * *

the journey was more

fun than where we ended

up

do you remember that night?

we hit every green light

from the turnpike to my

mom's house

we laughed so much that

night, all you wanted to do

was finish your tea

I think about that fun

drive all of the time

＊ ＊ ＊

long distance might

work as long as both

people are on the same

fucking page

we each have our books

but dammit the curriculum

didn't prepare us for the

emotional turmoil

        &

the extra credit never

brought up the

heartbreak

❋ ❋ ❋

his grandfather
died and I
was not allowed
to help him
grieve

I bet he still isn't
putting himself
first like
he should
be.

✻ ✻ ✻

so much missed

    waiting to be invited

    for you to be inspired

years of the same

i didn't mind it then

    but now i can't help

    but wonder

what could have changed

maybe all of it

MISSING POSTER

with your face on it

my number below

"please contact him

and tell him I still

long for him"

I leave a memory,

a light so you

know I'm waiting

for you back home

don't be afraid to

knock on the door

* * *

it's 2 am and I'm

crying to you, I

want my thoughts to

reach you as much as

I need to breathe.

it's 4 pm and I'm sobbing

thinking of the future

that was snatched away

I sit numb my

fingers tingling

my nails just want to

feel blood again

✳ ✳ ✳

"I will try"

      no

      don't

you can just

say no instead of

giving me a hope

that you will

soon crush

all I wanted to do

was love you

you were more than

okay with taking

my love

it changed when I

became self-sufficient

did you love me or the

fact that you took

care of me

* * *

if I knew the

last time we

locked lips

would be that

night

I would

have never come

up for air

I'd sooner die

than let you

go again

※ ※ ※

in my dreams you are
still loving
the look in your eye a
familiar one

when I wake up I want to
reach out to you
but your walls as high as they are,
I can't reach you directly

And my little arms can only
throw paper airplanes for
so long before I run out
of paper

* * *

I'm chasing the high
I felt when I was
with you

so many bad trips
unsupervised

nothing comes close to
the feelings I had
with you

If I had the chance
I'd overdose on you
and be okay with never
living again

* * *

how can you not
look me in the
eye

how can you keep
your emotions so
deep inside

I want your reaction
like the air I breathe
I just want to know
if you miss me
too

✳ ✳ ✳

I sometimes wish I kept my feelings inside

like I used to

I felt sad and scared but I didn't have to face my

feelings head on

I don't know how to shut the fuck up everyone has

ammo against me

But I like being vocal

I like people knowing when I'm upset

I love how my anger courses through me

reminding me that although all there is around me is

rain, my flame will not extinguish I will survive out of

SPITE

in spite of you and how you treated me and how you loved me

and made me cry and didn't fight for us

you're a fool

you never deserved me

i miss you

you were my whole life

and you took it

away from me

you just murdered my heart, the weapon

the love you finally

found for yourself

I heard you're letting

that self-love slip, be

careful, you just killed

me for

fun

when did my hatred

for you fade?

I see in your face, nostolgia

the memories clouded by

the aftermath of what you

did to me

I loved you once

* * *

five years to the day ago

there was no light in my soul

nothing worth living for

all I wanted was death

when you don't care whether

you live or die the people

around you try to help but

get sick of you fast

forgive me for using you to make

myself better

without you I'd be dead

someone else will reap the reward

that you worked so hard on

and that's okay

＊ ＊ ＊

I miss how familiar

you are

I miss my memories

with you

                because when

I bring them up it

stings

CHAPTER 3

full of rage

the same look of hatred

eyes darkened

you're okay with repeating

the past what

happened to changing

our fate

don't you remember

the blood

    tears

    the challenge of

keeping myself alive

* * *

self harmed in
many ways

begging for love
isolation
sex with strangers
starvation

you don't need a
blade to hurt yourself

the hate is more
than enough to
start

when I slice I

feel relief I feel

things other than

grief I feel wet

and rust I feel

ache and skin trying

to close I feel

more than

SADNESS when

I hurt myself I

feel

good.

＊　＊　＊

we're not supposed to

scratch we can't

bleed all the

months of being

clean will be ruined

if you don't control

your

SADNESS

and

ANGER

but the pain is nice

to feel, I'd rather

my skin torn up

than my heart.

* * *

empty pockets

empty hearts

empty smiles

empty eyes

all I am is empty space

✳ ✳ ✳

nose bleeds, is it because I'm

pushing myself too far?

I have to ignore the pain

and discomfort and go about

my day as if it was a

normal one

the diagnosis is not one I

wanted.

* * *

we're not friends

we never had the chance

to be friends

I don't want to be your friend

especially not right now.

my words come from

broken hearts

i write through the

tears and the pain

you took a piece of my

heart and so did he

now i'm running on

empty

✻ ✻ ✻

it's not that bad it
could be worse

sure its been 3 days
since I last showered

but it was bad before
i'd go a whole week

i'll be back on my
feet soon enough

the sun is out
to stay

＊　＊　＊

in order to survive the

unknown you must be polite

bare your fangs early and

fear retaliation

just stay quiet and pretty

and he'll go away

sooner or later

* * *

I'm sick in the head

under my skin

in the bed

filled with sin

from a past life, maybe

all I know is I don't

deserve it

now.

* * *

I know exactly what
I have to do but
a deer in the headlights
is what I
am

Will I ever get
my work done?
my mental health
depends on
it

❀ ❀ ❀

forced interactions

angry glances

     i don't want this

always around us

no moment of peace

     why is he higher

on the list of priorities

before him it was

     US vs THEM

now its you two vs

me

don't fall for me,
you said. and I
shrugged, and
relieved that you
said that so early
so that I could
quickly move on.

I thought I

could handle you but

then you disappeared...

when you came back

I had already

burned the bridge.

You would have

drowned if you

had tried

again

(#6)

✳ ✳ ✳

fun. same size.

sarcastic. to the point.

always drinking. always

working. fun. downtown.

drunk. missed. drunk.

wednesday. forgotten. missed.

drunk.

(#9)

* * *

you didn't stop

when

I

    said

        no.

immature but fun

to be around.

those who harm are human too.

(#11)

✻ ✻ ✻

I wish your

mind was as solid as your body.

I thought you

needed time alone.

I can't be in a

room without reflections.

I love myself too

much.

(#12)

✻ ✻ ✻

Beautiful!

why did it take so long?
you didn't want more
which is fine!

just know when I think
of you

it's nothing but nice
things
(#13)

* * *

don't play with

people's hearts! why

didn't she give me a

warning when she KNEW

your plan? Fuck my

joy in the moment,

think of my happiness

for LIFE!

(#14)

＊ ＊ ＊

we like guys

with meat on their

bones and can take

care of themselves

and know how to

clean

      not you

(#16)

how confusing you
were

you act, say different
you got what you wanted
why didn't you
return the favor
or
my shirt?

a muse, amazing
a lover? the worst.
(#17)

you don't believe

in God yet my

friends and I are

going to hell because

we aren't actually girls?

other than that,

good luck.

(#23)

❋　❋　❋

"I want a FWB
thing with you"

I thought about it
for a long while

then decided I
was worthy of
love and a
title
(#25)

✳ ✳ ✳

is it too much to hope
that it'll be different with
me?

am I naive to believe that
you will treat me right?

your past, revealed- I want
to ignore it

maybe it'll be different
with me?

or maybe a waste of time

＊ ＊ ＊

how will ___ learn

to love ___ if I'm

the only one holding

the conversation?

give me something to

work with!

floodgates open

        hold on to hope

you know the trek by heart

        I expect a change

        a difference

you'll get hurt at the same bend

        but why do I

you can't sail with hope

you'll fall into frigid seas

        all I give is what I want in

        return

do they deserve it

        irrelevent

        I do.

✳ ✳ ✳

oh...

that's what I said but

what I wanted to say was

you can't be out here saying

you don't want to love me when

all of your actions say

otherwise.

a toothbrush immediatly

loving glances and giggles

encouraging my affection

making promises

men will tell you what you want

to hear without fail

and you'll feel like a

fool

＊ ＊ ＊

attention is

    addicting

juggling is a good

time until you

get tired

    who should

I let fall?

* * *

you're a liar

at least until

I figure out your

intentions with

me.

every kind word

from your mouth,

every loving glance

will be treated like

fiction until I

have all the facts

I need.

I didn't take you for an

idiot

until you let me go

only a fool would see

a treasure so stunning

and walk away

empty handed.

✳ ✳ ✳

I've got your back,*

*as long as you're

    single

        unhappy

    questioning

       alone

If you've got mine*

* * *

you only think of me

when you're drunk

you're always drunk

I would love you back

in my life but only

if you're sober

* * *

my heart dropped to

my stomach when

I saw the smoke

escape your lips

I panicked and

snatched the cigarette

I threw and stomped

on it without thinking

I'd rather you get

addicted to

me.

I don't feel guilty
for what I did

If you were in my
shoes, you would have
done the same

You're aware of my
needs and my
selfishness

Don't get lazy
I move on quick.

＊　＊　＊

you have the nerve

the audacity

the balls

but you are

definitely

lacking in the

brain department

so many other trees

in the forest and you're

pining after me?

taken an axe to that heart

destroy the branches

weighing you down

start a fire

for someone else

* * *

"this is karma"

you said it not I

you knew you

deserved the

pain, you saw it

coming both times

at first I was sad

to make you

suffer and then

I remembered that

you deserve

to

* * *

you didn't

have permission

to share that

information you

took a plan of

attack straight

into the enemy

ranks if you

are not for

me

then

DIE

❄   ❄   ❄

don't go into the jungle without

protection

tigers claw at my chest, leaving

me ragged out of breath

wondering why did I walk in

here expecting a nice stroll

it's hard to stalk prey when

the prey is an apex predator

I have the upper hand

dangling from a branch far

above your head

you look me dead in the eye your

grin curdling my blood

I am going to fall into the

belly of the beast

and its all my fault

heed my warning,

don't go into the jungle

on your own

* * *

we just keep running back into

the hand that would

rather strike than feed us

mean people aren't at the

start, they season you

well before sticking you in

the pot

its hard to remember your worth

when you're ripped and thrown

like loose change on the sidewalk

* * *

dreams set aside

for what?

to survive.

I have but all of time to bide

have you an idea

of what it is to

starve?

I hunger for ambition

to return to my soul

to be able to follow

what I long for

* * *

I didn't sleep well that night
your arm under my head
made me fear you going
numb.

I forget how hard it was for
me to learn to open up
and I'm sorry I wasn't there
for you.

I just had my own bullshit
to deal with and I didn't
wanna drown trying to save
someone
else.

the phone rang and the person on the other
end matters more to me than you

a very hard month. she just wanted to release
steam and speak to someone she trusts

I was heavily affected by the events that
occurred, and the talk was good to have

I mentioned all of this to you that day.

the way you looked at me with my headphones
on. you were annoyed and it showed

you were acting like you understood but you

sure as hell wanted the attention for yourself

tapping your foot, mouthing "is she done yet?" and

making noise with your loud sighs.

don't wonder why I didn't try to see you again.

* * *

you were promised

devotion

obedience

and love

you walked away the first time

and I'm walking away

this time.

* * *

trauma isn't a competition

but if you really think

you've survived as much

as me

you're not only a fool

you don't know me as well

as you claim to

✼ ✼ ✼

I feel everything

    all at once or not

        at all.

there is no gray in my

    world, only green

        and black.

everyday I wake up hoping

    that it won't be the

        end.

where do I put my expectations

    my hopes and

        dreams?

i just want to be happy.

※ ※ ※

the bruises you left on my body
didn't hurt as much as the
bruises you left on my heart

I didn't mean to cry that hard
especially in front of you
I wanted to comfort you but instead
you ended up holding me

its so easy to talk to you, and I'll admit
that I got ahead of myself, especially
when I gave so much attention to you
and you gave me none

it wasn't your fault, I understand that
but you'll be leaving again and
I need to move on

I hate talking to you I don't
like the way you make me
feel
        like shit like
        I'm not smart
        like
        I only talk about
        how sad my life is

IT IS SAD

im scared hungry lonely cold
and I'm doing it on

MY OWN

my stomach hurts now in

this moment because

as much as I want to

cut you off I want to

help you find your humanity

but at the risk of losing

my own?

✻ ✻ ✻

your actions don't match
what you are saying

your hand is on my waist,
let me pull away from you
please

i miss when we used to talk about
the sky and where we would go
next, now you go on about
your conquests of sex

what are your true intentions
you were so interested in being
my friend?

what does that word even

mean to you?

you want more from me, I

want less time with you.

* * *

First hand experience

     pretty hurts

makes it easy to stop trying

     don't waste time

     actively trying to get

     hurt

how can you leave paintings up, the
same ones that bring you pain

the memories now bittersweet,
don't hold on in vain.

aesthetic makes no sense.

* * *

what makes you think

for even a moment

that you are allowed

back into my life?

you never even TRIED to

be my friend and yet

you want to pretend

that what you did to

me never even happened

its my fault you come

crawling back, I know the

effect I have on

men

just let me bury the

hatchet, don't attempt

amends

you're a what if

that didn't have a chance to happen

CHAPTER 4

not looking, just alone

＊ ＊ ＊

short

sweet

and to the point

you won't find

another like

me

* * *

what do you call

a server who

doesn't clean their tables

doesn't deliver their food

and doesn't check on guests?

shitty.

* * *

find a spot just

for two, highest

peak overlooking

the range and

SCREAM

give your voice to

the wind, the trees

and let it go for

just a moment

✳ ✳ ✳

footsteps sound
different when it
rains, when you're
near a river, and when
you're covered in dirt

different terrain
than what you're
used to

give it a try

＊　＊　＊

we came for moonshine

and stayed for the

mountains

a natural beauty, a

challenge conquered

Thank you Mother

for your creation

we should all spend

more time outdoors

✿ ✿ ✿

the sky is a lovely

shade of green

while the sun comes

up

not enough to become

my new favorite color

but

only time will

tell

the same blood between

us

different lives

    docile creature

compared to the

hurricane you are

you are awe inspiring

one of a kind

✳ ✳ ✳

I tend to jump

into the pool too

soon after eating

I can't help it I

love the way the

water feels cool against

my skin

I shiver but I'm

reminded I am

alive.

✽　✽　✽

how come we have

to pay to see the

ocean?

there's so much of

it out there and

you're telling me

you make money

off of something

that belongs to all

of us?

＊　＊　＊

you've been a blessing

but it seems only

to me

your sin: a sloth

you're late, behind

schedule, why

are you so

SLOOOOOOOOOOOW

don't mess anything

else up, Dorian,

I'll come for you

✻ ✻ ✻

i'm not supposed to

talk to you

but even if I

was able to

I still wouldn't

because you

are someone

that is not to be

trusted.

＊　＊　＊

hands shaking

alone in the cold

at 9 in the morning

refuge! a fire,

small but warm

keeping me alive

huddled close, I look

embarassing but I

sigh with relief

I can feel again

✻ ✻ ✻

isn't it awful how much smaller

the world gets

when you meet a new

friend

I find it pretty neat

＊ ＊ ＊

you are 6000 miles

beneath me

the air is thin and

I'm light headed

as if we were in

the same room.

you're missing out

※ ※ ※

i miss your hands

soft, strong firm

I ache for the hands

that were experts

in breaking my

bones. the air

escaping from

the dark. scared

but longing for

the crack

(about the chiropractor)

CHAPTER 5

The One?

unspoken promises

between us

who will be the first to

admit that they're

in love?

* * *

let me love you the only way I

know how

with reckless abandon, drowing

you with the affection that

you have never gotten and

will never get again when

I'm

gone

I wish I could love
my self as hard
as I love you

I'm working on it

* * *

I'm not good at

keeping secrets

I want to

scream

from

the top of

my lungs that

I'm in love with

you

✳ ✳ ✳

every new experience

is one

I

would rather do

with

you

✽ ✽ ✽

why can't I
sleep?

has it always
been this hard
to sleep

without you?

come home soon
I'm so tired

* * *

my passion for you

doesn't dwindle

while you're gone

I'm a hopeless romantic

but you take the cake!

what a wonderful place

to make me yours

it may have rained but

your nervous smile kept

my heart warm and dry

if you want me

to take my time

to love, you should

probably not be

so easy to love!

I'd burn every bridge

in the world if it

meant keeping this

flame between us

alive

I want to be selfish

I want what I have

given so willingly

I want to be loved

without question

or restraint

I want to be loved

by you

* * *

I don't want you

to miss

me

at all I want you

in my

arms

I'll be home soon

so don't

let

me

go

❋ ❋ ❋

Finally!

    A worthy opponent.

Someone appreciative

of this

    battle

String your bow,

    beware my

    arrow

I'm armed with

love

✺ ✺ ✺

I want to hold you

to my body to

let you feel that you are

safe

your frame, much longer

than I

your grief outweighs

my own

you've been strong

for so long

take a rest with me.

❋ ❋ ❋

intense emotion

felt at once

fear to vocalize

desire for devotion

intimidating glance

you have me paralyzed

thank you for saying it

first

I want to get closer

I made direct eye contact

I stroked your arm

you are a snail?

read my body language

I WANT YOU

written all over me

ah yes, show me what

those hands do

I need a closer look

and there's a spot for me right

on your lap

Printed in the United States
by Baker & Taylor Publisher Services